A GIFT FOR:

_____

FROM:

_____

Design by Melissa Gerber
Typography: Garamond, Growler Script, Heavenfield Typewriter, Lulo Clean One, Marvellous Bold, Minik Bold, MrsEaves Italic,
MrsEaves Roman, Poetica Small Caps, Rebel, and Trade Gothic Condensed No. 18
All images used under official license from Shutterstock.com.

ISBN: 978-1-63059-847-1
BOK1535

Made in China
0320

LIFE STARTS AT
Retirement

By Lou Harry

CONTENTS

$\int$NTRODUCTION

Welcome to retirement, a time when you could simply increase your time in front of the television or, instead, experience the world in ways you've been dreaming about all of your life.

Your choice.

Since you have this book in your hands, let's assume that you prefer the latter option, the one that involves new experiences, joys, and discoveries mixed with the best of those things you long-loved but never had enough time to do.

So let the games...and the travel...and the complete control of your choices begin. Approach the coming years as a series of amazing opportunities.

A Beginner's Bucket List

Your bucket list—the things you want to do while still on this earth—is likely to be very different from anyone else's. Here's a customizable helper to create your own to-do list.

1. The one place I want to see that I've never been to is

_____

2. I would like to spend more time hanging out with

_____

3. The one thing I'd like to change about myself—that I realistically could change—is

_____

4. The one thing I should apologize for is _____ and the person I should apologize to is

_____

5. The skill I wish I'd learned and would like to acquire is

_____

6. The sport or game I would most like to learn is

_____

7. The living musician I've enjoyed most but have not seen live yet is

_____

8. The household skill I believe I can improve on—and enjoy—the most is

_____

9. The living person from my past who I'd most like to thank for his or her influence on my life is

_____

10. The person whose life I could most positively impact in the upcoming year is

_____

11. One thing in my house that I can upgrade that would bring me the most ongoing pleasure is

_____

12. The one item on this list that I can act on TODAY is

_____

"RETIREMENT
IS LIKE A LONG
VACATION IN
Las Vegas.
THE GOAL IS TO
ENJOY IT TO THE
FULLEST, BUT
NOT SO FULLY
THAT YOU RUN
OUT OF MONEY."

—JONATHAN CLEMENTS

GOING PLACES

Yes, it's a great time to think about the places you've been. But it's also a great time to add to that list by hitting the road. And that "road" could lead you around the world or simply to another part of town.

EXPLORE THE NATIONAL PARKS.

The biggest one is Wrangell-St. Elias in Alaska, covering over eight million acres. The smallest is the Thaddeus Kosciuszko National Memorial in Pennsylvania, covering only .02 acres. In between is a wide array of national parks just waiting for you to explore. Whatever path you choose, there's a good chance that you'll find a collector—someone whose goal is to get to every one of these national treasures. You don't have to be quite so ambitious, given that there's at least one national park in every state of the union, plus the District of Columbia, American Samoa, Guam, Puerto Rico, and the Virgin Islands.

*G*O HOSTELING.

Many people know of hostels as places where young people crash while taking a year off in Europe before diving into college. But hostels are also scattered around the U.S., offering clean but sometimes barracks-like conditions for those traveling on a tight budget. Want to see the country—or the world—but really only need a bed and a shared bathroom? Have little concerns about privacy? Consider joining the throngs that are heading to hostels.

Who is the most interesting person you've ever met while travelling?

14

LEARN ABOUT WHERE YOU LIVE.

You've spent much of your life on the job. The side effect of that is often exhaustion over the weekends and vacations often spent elsewhere. That can add up to little time to explore your own town. Whether that means a native New Yorker finally going to the top of the Empire State Building or a small town Iowan making a first trip to the local historical society, getting a better sense of place can lead to more civic pride and greater social opportunities.

Find your local Visitors Bureau's list of top attractions or a local publication's best restaurants. How many have you visited?

EXPAND YOUR GOLF HORIZONS.

Now is your chance to take your clubs beyond your local club and hit those courses you've long dreamed of playing. *Golf Digest* offers a convenient ranking of the 100 greatest public golf courses. And they are all over the country, including West Virginia's 100-year-old (and recently restored) The Greenbrier; Texas' gentle and serene Omni Barton Creek; and the timeless Donald Ross course at French Lick Resort in Indiana. Just try to keep your eye on the ball when playing the Pebble Beach holes that overlook California's crashing surf.

What's a course on your wish list that's less than 300 miles away? How about anywhere in the world?

ONE-ON-ONE TIME WITH GRANDKIDS.

Family vacations are great. But don't pass up opportunities to create one-on-one time with your grandkids. Take a grandparent/grandchild day trip, overnighter, or weekend jaunt. Whether it's to Walt Disney World or a local campground, it will not be forgotten...by either your grandchild or the no-doubt-appreciative parents who, thanks to you, can have a little vacation of their own.

What is your favorite memory of a grandparent?

ONE-ON-ONE TIME WITH YOUR SIBLINGS, KIDS, COUSINS, ETC.

When was the last time you had the pleasure of hanging out with just your brother? Or your favorite cousin? Now you don't have to give up a family vacation in order to spend quality time with special individuals in your life. That could mean a weekend at the lake, a museum-hopping trip to the big city, or just a nice visit with plenty of gabbing time on the front porch.

CONTINUAL CRUISING.

Some people dream of vacationing on a cruise ship. With your schedule suddenly unbound by workplace commitments, you can take advantage of seasonal offers, make spontaneous decisions, and head out to sea as often as you can afford. Rumors have flown that actually living on a cruise ship full-time is cheaper than an assisted living facility…and some have tried it: Witness the BBC story about an 89-year-old woman who was a permanent resident of the *Queen Elizabeth II*. But putting aside the need to disembark and reboard regularly, plus the challenges of living out of a suitcase, you also have to figure in the difficulties of acquiring insurance and ongoing medical care. Instead of the fantasy, though, enjoy the reality of a few extra cruises a year if you don't mind the off-season and interior cabins.

If you were to go away for six months with two suitcases, what would you pack?

GO CAMPING.

The great outdoors can be even greater in retirement when you don't have to be back to the office on Monday, especially if the leaves are turning, the fish are biting, and there are still a few brats to cook over the fire. Many the retiree has found an additional group of friends at a campground, forming a true, technology-less social network. More introverted? There's no place better than the woods to get away from it all (just request a campsite far from the playground or pool).

What's your favorite food that can be cooked over a campfire?

HAVE AN RV ADVENTURE.

Whether you want to invest in one or simply rent, an RV can be a great way to hit the road, see the country, and not worry about whether the hotel is going to be worth the money. Yes, these beasts are gas-guzzlers. But you'll never have trouble finding a restroom, and having a kitchenette certainly saves money on food.

HIKE.

The shortest distance between two points, we learned in geometry class, is a straight line between them. But that's not necessarily the most fun route, as anyone who has hiked can tell you. Whether you are exploring urban neighborhoods or taking a trek through the great outdoors, finding new routes can take you—mentally and physically—to unexpected places. Walk with a partner or friend and you'll find pleasure not only in the conversation, but also the comfortable silences. On your own, it's a chance to think deeply and see the world from a different angle.

EXTENDED TRAVEL.

Remember the days of squeezing a vacation into your limited time off from work? Trying to compare the cost of air travel vs. the lost time it would take to go by car? With greater flexibility—for instance, finding the cheapest time to fly and using the savings for extra hotel nights—you might find that you can actually save money by extending your trip. For extra comfort, don't just add up the expenses when figuring the cost of a trip, but consider what you would spend if you were home.

WING IT.

Another way to save when it comes to vacation can come from deciding not on where you can go, but by what's available at a lower cost. Again, your flexibility is key here. But if you don't have strings, why not take advantage of a cheap flight to Vegas or an off-peak cruise? And resort towns can be lovely in the slightly off-seasons when the attractions are still open but the crowds have thinned.

MAKE A PILGRIMAGE.

What's that one place you've always dreamed of visiting? For some, it might be the Louvre in Paris. For others, it may be the Baseball Hall of Fame in Cooperstown, New York. For still others, it might be the place where your great-grandparents settled. Whatever the case, this is the time to get to these bucket list places, making sure to give yourself time not just to see the sites, but to soak up the fact that you've finally made it there after all these years.

If you won a trip to anywhere in the world, where would you go?

10 Questions
TO ASK YOURSELF
BEFORE TRAVELING

Before you go too far, ask yourself the
following questions to get a better sense
of where to go, with whom, and when.

1. How much flexibility do you like when traveling? Do you prefer a pre-planned tour experience complete with guide or would you rather be left to your own devices?

2. What's your driving tolerance? Would you prefer having the control of your own vehicle or would you rather take public transportation?

3. Do you like to eat what you are familiar with or take chances on local fare?

4. How much of the experience is just for you and how much is for the person you are traveling with?

5. How flexible are you about accommodations?

6. Do you like to be left alone or would you prefer to meet locals and interact with fellow travelers?

7. How much room do you want to leave in your suitcase to bring back souvenirs and other purchases?

8. Do you prefer the authentic or experiences created for the entertainment of tourists? For some, Walt Disney World is a dream come true, for instance; for others, it's not even a vacation.

9. How will your medical needs or physical limitations impact the trip you are planning?

10. Would you rather be on your feet or spending more time with your toes in the sand?

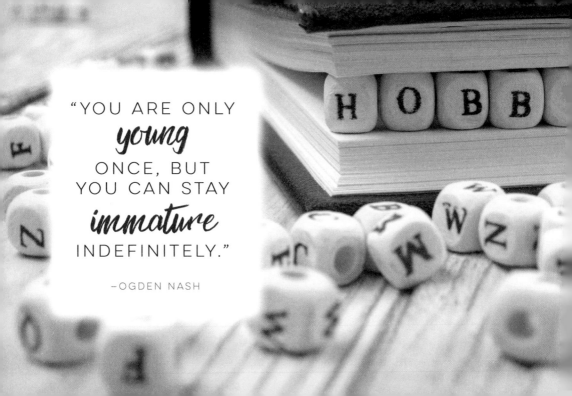

"YOU ARE ONLY *young* ONCE, BUT YOU CAN STAY *immature* INDEFINITELY."

–OGDEN NASH

HOBBY UPGRADES

Retirement is the right time to plunge deeper into your already existing interests, to discover new ones, or both. And no need to squeeze those pleasures into precious weekend time. Now you can get lost for hours in the things you love to do.

ATTEND A CONVENTION OR CONFERENCE.

Depending on your career, you may have attended conventions in the past—ones that focused on your profession, whether that was hardware wholesaling or consumer electronics. Now is your chance to go to a convention purely for the fun of it. How about Comic Con in San Diego? Or Gen Con, the board game gathering in Indianapolis that attracts over 30,000 players. If you are a cigar aficionado, a model train hobbiest, a part-time Santa Claus, a fan of Jane Austen's books, or a baseball card collector, there's a gathering just waiting for you.

If you could attend a gathering of people with a love of one thing, what would it be?

ING.

If the occasional karaoke night in a local bar doesn't satisfy your urge to sing out, consider joining a local chorus or choir. Provided you can hit a note or two, you can expect to be welcomed. If you lean toward the sacred music, check in with your local places of worship—many don't require you to be either a member of the congregation or even a believer in that particular faith in order to sing praises. If you are looking for something more secular, many cities have men's and women's choruses, or mixed groups. Meetup.com is a good place to start your search but local arts councils can help as well.

MAKE SOME ART.

Legendary American folk artist Grandma Moses (aka Anna Mary Robertson Moses) didn't start painting until she was in her 70s. So there's no shame in waiting until retirement to focus some of your attention on the act of creating art. There are commercial studios where wine and painting mix, and art centers with full slates of classes in everything from ceramics and printmaking to digital photography and metalsmithing. And you don't have to be in a degree program to take a class or four at a local art college.

What items are hanging on your walls that were either made by you or made by people you know?

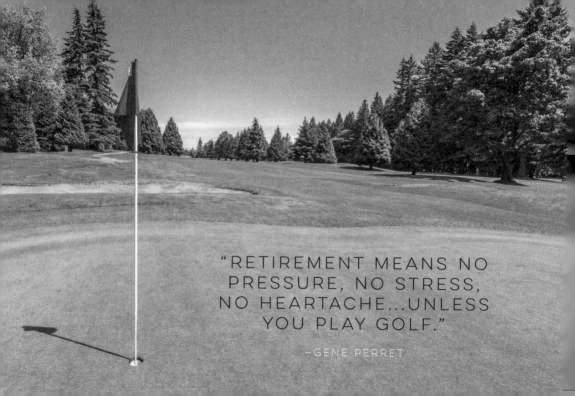

"RETIREMENT MEANS NO
PRESSURE, NO STRESS,
NO HEARTACHE...UNLESS
YOU PLAY GOLF."

–GENE PERRET

IMPROVE YOUR GOLF GAME.

At last, a chance to shave a few points off of your score! Any serious or semi-serious golfer knows that improvement comes with practice. Well, now you have the time to get out on the links and do just that. Of course, conversation could be more challenging if you are heading out with the same foursome a few days a week rather than your old once-a-month-or-less schedule.

If you could ask a golf pro for help with one aspect of your game, what would it be?

CREATE IN THE KITCHEN.

The days of coming home and scrambling to figure out what's for dinner (and resorting to microwavable something from the freezer) can also retire now that you have time to actually craft your meals. Make use of tips you've picked up from the Food Network. Dig out those yellowing recipes you clipped from magazines. Or you can just go to Supercook.com, check off boxes for the ingredients you have at home, and get recipes that won't require a trip to the supermarket.

GET COMPETITIVE WITH YOUR COOKING.

Want to challenge your cooking skills even further? State and county fairs around the country hold cooking competitions where piemakers and fried chicken perfectionists battle it out. North Carolina's fair includes a one-pot sweet potato contest while a local beekeepers association hosts a cooking-with-honey challenge at the State Fair of Texas. Or you can enter in your zip code at the International Chili Society's website to find a chili cook-off near you.

Putting modesty aside, what is the one thing that you are exceptionally good at making?

BRING FAVORITE GAMES TO THE TABLE AGAIN.

Remember the pleasures of marathon games of Monopoly? Or those strategic Scrabble battles of yore? While those games have spun seemingly endless spinoffs, the basic versions are still around and available cheap. The advantage of such oldies but goodies? It's unlikely you'll have to explain the rules to anyone. (Unless you truly play by the Monopoly rules, which means none of that "putting money on the Free Parking space" nonsense.)

What game did you love playing as a kid? When was the last time you played it?

LEARN NEW GAMES.

Monopoly, Risk, and Scrabble are great. But there's plenty more on the game front to explore. Yes, you can embrace new technology and engage yourself in video games and online challenges. But nothing beats a good tabletop game where you are playing face-to-face across the table from your opponents. If you haven't tried anything fresher than Yahtzee, consider the popular board game Ticket to Ride, which has become a contemporary classic over the past decade with its strategic-but-easy-to-understand game play involving building networks of railroads across the country. Catan (formerly Settlers of Catan) is another recent addition to the canon of great board games. Meetup.com can guide you toward game groups, and you can find friendly local game stores across the country that offer games to sample and host introductory sessions as well as competitions.

*B*LOG.

If the idea of starting a blog sounds intimidating, take a look at the length and frequency of your Facebook posts or the quality of your Instagram page. In other words, you may already be doing it, just not calling it a blog. Launching a blog allows you to write and present whatever you want without an editor over your shoulder (which can be a good or bad thing). You can pick a single topic of interest or be a generalist. Point potential readers to your blog through other channels (Facebook, Twitter, etc.), and make sure to comment on other people's blogs and newsfeeds with a link to your site. At minimum, a blog can be a great way to exercise your writing skills and let people know what's on your mind. At best, you may find yourself with a following. Easy and cheap tools to start your own blog are available via www.wordpress.com and lots of other sites.

What do you most often post about on social media?

CATCH THAT FISH.

Fishing is a patience game. And now that you have the time, you can work on becoming patient enough to wait for the big one. You can also expand your fishing horizons, going beyond the local watering hole to places where the fish are more likely to bite. Fishing is also a great way to spend quality time with old friends who appreciate both the conversation and the silence that comes with the sport.

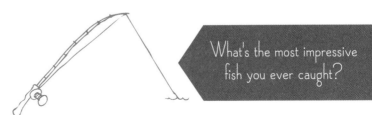

What's the most impressive fish you ever caught?

JOIN/FORM A BAND.

Got a garage, some music skills, and some like-minded friends? Whether your tastes lean to jazz, folk, rap, or rock, you now have the time to actually practice. Worried about your lack of experience? Remember that the less you have, the wider the pool of peers you can choose from to round out your band's sound. Advice from Metal Method, an online resource of guitar lessons: Find the musicians first—a lead singer can wait. Just make sure to warn your neighbors if you'll be practicing in your garage.

What
music truly
makes you
happy?

*B*E CRAFTY.

Rather than trying to slip your knitting, crocheting, and needlepointing into your worklife, you now have the time for either big projects or lots of small ones. Perhaps you are a newcomer and finally ready to commit some time to learning these skills. In that case, there are a host of websites and, likely, local shops eager to welcome you into the craft. Just remember that cost saving shouldn't be your prime motivator. Most things you can make can be bought cheaper. But no store-bought item rivals the pride of creation or the likelihood to become a family heirloom as something you've created with your own hands.

When was the last time you tried a new art or craft?

GET TO THE FINAL LEVEL OF A VIDEO GAME.

Okay, so it shouldn't be one of your major life goals, but there's a unique satisfaction to making it to the last level on a challenging video game. And before you scoff that video games are on the fringe of entertainment, keep in mind that *Game Informer*, the magazine at the center of the business, is the fourth highest circulating print publication in the country. And not all of those are twentysomethings in their parents' basement.

GET COMPETITIVE.

If you think you've got game and want to test your skills, there's
no shortage of opportunities. Of course, casinos across the
country—and many a rec room—host poker tournaments. The
advantage to these over cash games is that they start with a level
playing field. But don't limit yourself to gambling. You can find
Scrabble tournaments, trivia tournaments, and who knows!
You may find yourself heading to the Backgammon, Go, or
Mahjong World Championships. But outdoor games can bring
competitive fun as well, whether that's stereotypical senior games
like shuffleboard and bocce, or more active sports like tennis
and racquetball.

UPGRADE YOUR GARDEN.

During your work years, you need to set aside time for gardening. Now there are more opportunities to tinker, prune, and upgrade. Of course, it can become harder to do the bending and digging that expansive outdoor gardening can require, so consider a shift in strategy that includes lower-maintenance plants in the main garden supplemented by potted perennials. Take the time to mulch to avoid weed growth. And remember that there are tools with ergonomic handles so that those with arthritis might still be able to enjoy gardening.

TRY STAND-UP COMEDY/IMPROVISATION.

If you've been told for years that you're the funniest person in the room, how about testing your skills on stage? Most comedy clubs have a dedicated open mic night when would-be comics can try their best bits for five minutes or so. If you prefer comedy with more give-and-take, and are comfortable with spontaneity, improvisation groups hold classes with some also offering weekly improvisation game nights where amateurs can try out in a friendly environment. Whichever route you choose, remember that a silent audience doesn't mean you aren't funny. Performing comedy for an audience of strangers requires a skill set that comes from practice.

Top 10 Hobbies
YOU SHOULD CONSIDER

Now that you have the time, why not branch out and try something new? Just as you stepped out of the cubicle, step out of the box here and who knows?

1. Acting. You may be surprised at how much of a shortage there can be of older adult talent at community theaters and even at some semi-pro and professional ones.

2. Woodworking. In this age of IKEA—where DIY can mean using a hex key to turn a few screws—honest, authentic woodworking is becoming a rarity. Cleaning out the garage and making room for a few pieces of equipment could bring enormous satisfaction, plus some useful furniture and memorable gifts.

3. Other arts and crafts. Needlepoint and crocheting are great, but how about trying to make stained glass or a cozy rug?

4. Swimming. Hitting the pool is not only pleasurable, but it's also a great way to minimize the effects of osteoarthritis, especially if land-based exercise is painful.

5. Taking up a musical instrument. It's never too late to start learning an instrument. And in addition to being able to serenade your sweetheart, there are other benefits. Music has been credited with helping uncover forgotten memories just through the sheer act of focusing on music.

6. Dancing. Whether it's ballroom, tap, or tango, dancing is not just great for the feet and legs. The mental agility involved in following steps can help keep the mind sharp. Plus you can't argue with the social benefits.

7. Restoration. Whether it's fixing electronics, repairing lawn equipment, tinkering with old watches, or bringing new luster to jewelry, there's great psychological benefit to be had from knowing that you took something that might have been thrown away and given it new life.

8. Editorialize. You've got opinions. Everyone in your family knows you have opinions. So why not try to articulate them in print? Letters to the editor are good places to start—with the rise of social media, fewer people are actually sending letters to publications, which increase the chance of yours being published. Generate some conversation and then start pitching to the op-ed section. Those skills from your high school debate team could come in handy.

9. Food club. No, not fight club. Dining is as talked about these days as movies and TV. And new eateries are popping up on a regular basis. While, by all means, you should stay true to an old favorite, how about leading a weekly, bi-weekly, or monthly jaunt to someplace new? Call ahead and ask if your gang can talk to the chef for additional fun and insight.

10. Outdoor volunteering. Your local Department of Natural Resources can tip you off with volunteer opportunities in your area. That could mean loon watching in Minnesota, butterfly counting in Indiana, or any of many other unexpected excuses to get out for a walk while helping local wildlife.

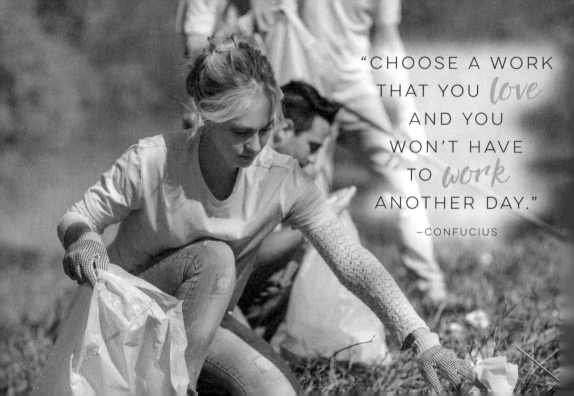

"CHOOSE A WORK THAT YOU *love* AND YOU WON'T HAVE TO *work* ANOTHER DAY."

–CONFUCIUS

THE GREATER GOOD

It's never too late to make the world a better place. That can mean upgrading your neighborhood or traveling to parts unknown to improve the planet. Projects large and small—and some you may think of yourself— are waiting for you.

$\mathcal{S}$IGN UP FOR THE PEACE CORPS.

Good news, do-gooders. There is no upper age limit when applying to the Peace Corps. Most assignments require a four-year degree, but there are some exceptions based on prior work experience. If you have a medical or nursing license, there may be even more opportunities through their Response and Global Health Service Partnership programs.

Where in the world would you like to make a positive impact?
What skills and experience could you bring to the table?

AID ANIMALS.

There's a good boy—a lot of good boys—just waiting for you to take them for a walk. Their sisters are waiting too. And their feline friends. They are the residents of your local ASPCA, Humane Society, or other animal shelter, and such facilities can always use a helping hand (or paw). It can be as little as a few hours a week but, of course, the risk is that you'll want to take many of these furry friends home. If bigger or more varied beasts bring you bliss, look for volunteer opportunities at your local zoo.

What are some programs that your faith institution is involved with that you think are making the biggest difference in the lives of people in your community? How could they be improved?

BE FAITHFUL.

For many, one visit a week to a place of worship is enough. But churches, mosques, synagogues, and other faith institutions have a lot more going on than just religious services. They serve as bustling activity centers with educational offerings, charitable efforts, and lots of social opportunities. Being involved can begin with taking a class or attending a meeting, and can grow to joining the board as a member, participating in clergy search committees, helping with daycare, cooking for holiday meals, and much more.

*G*ET POLITICAL.

Want to help change the world or change your neighborhood? Helping the government go out with the old or in with the new—or helping keep the good ones in office—can truly impact your life and the lives of those around you. It's not just about elections, though. Your political action can be issue-oriented as well by helping a cause or priority you believe in get the attention of election officials, the media, and the public. Warning: There is a rabbit hole aspect to working in politics. Once you get known as a skillful, smart, dedicated volunteer, you may find yourself being encouraged to increase your participation with eventual encouragement to…

... RUN FOR OFFICE.

You've spent a lifetime watching other people make questionable political decisions. Perhaps news channels are on your radio presets and your TV default is a 24-hour news channel. Now may be the time to step up and make use of your experience and knowledge to compete for a local elected position. An ability to connect with people in a sociable way (and remember their names), speak to groups, and be open to ideas certainly can make a difference. And let's not underestimate the need—and the skills required—to raise money for a campaign. As the song says, "this land was made for you and me"—so why not help run it?

What are items that you treasure that were passed down to you from previous generations?

*P*URGE AND DONATE.

Retirement is a great opportunity to separate the items you really want to live with (and maintain) and those you can do without—something particularly important if you plan on downsizing. While you may consistently donate old clothes to your local Goodwill or other charity thrift shop already, there are other items you may find in your purge that could also have a better home elsewhere. While going through your photo collection, for instance, be aware of context in older photos. The historical society of your hometown— whether you still live there or not—may have a use for some of your images in their collection, whether that includes a long-gone local park, a restaurant that has undergone renovations, or a public event. Many such archives post their needs on their pages. No longer have use for some tabletop appliances? Check with local relief organizations that may be able to find a home for them to be put to good use. Local community centers may help you find places that would appreciate anything from books to sports equipment. (Alas, you are unlikely to find anyone willing to take your old 8-track tapes.)

*J*OIN A BOARD.

Your expertise, time, and financial support can be of enormous value to a nonprofit. As you select who you want to work with, Idealistcareers.org recommends three key steps:

1. Identify your strengths and skill sets. Think about what you can bring to an organization.

2. Determine the type of organization you want to affiliate with. For starters, taking a look at where you've allocated charitable donations in the past.

3. Put yourself out there.

That last step can mean active networking but don't be shy about contacting an organization directly. Idealist and other sites list organizations looking for such assistance.

What are three local organizations that you believe you could be of genuine service to? If you don't have an answer, what are three that you'd like to learn more about?

Close-Up:
ENCORES

What do Michael Jordan, Muhammad Ali, Roger Clemens, Wilt Chamberlain, Brett Favre, Allen Iverson, Magic Johnson, Mario Lemieux, George Foreman, and Pelé have in common?

They all retired and then came back for an encore.

Now, they may not have gotten to the same heights they reached in their primes. But they did prove that retirement need not be permanent, even when the chosen field is bone-crunching.

On the entertainment side, Jay Z announced that 2003's *The Black Album* would be his last. He put out another one three years later. Barbra Streisand retired from performing publicly in 2000...and has had two world tours since then. Three years after her Farewell tour, Cher was back on stage in Las Vegas. Audrey Hepburn retired just a few years after *My Fair Lady* but returned in the 1970s for *Robin and Marian*. Frank Sinatra said he was out in 1971, only to get back in by 1973. And after his last leading role in 1961, James Cagney returned to the screen twenty years later in *Ragtime*.

And let's not forget Theodore Roosevelt, who said he would never run again after his second term as President of the United States. That was 1909. By 1912, he was running again.

Top 10 Philanthropic
WAYS TO LEND A HAND

Retirement may be the right time to tighten your belt. It also may be a time when you have the ability to increase your charitable giving. Here are ten tips to keep in mind when it comes to being philanthropic.

1. Think about your priorities. While you may want to be generous, you can't help everyone and every cause. And don't obsess about how charities compare to each other. What problem do YOU want your money to help alleviate? Whether it's the arts, education, civic beautification, or anything else, keep in mind that there's no wrong answer.

2. Beware of scams. Unfortunately, there are folks out there who want to take advantage of your generosity. No donation is so urgent that you can't take the time to do some research. Be cautious of sound-alike names and don't just go to a suggested website to check; use other sources. And never give your social security number, bank account number, or other personal information that a legit charity would never request.

3. Don't judge a charity entirely by the percentage it claims goes to the cause. Instead, look at the results. Having a professional organization of decently paid staffers can lead to improved results and while that may lower the percentage of your donation that directly helps, it may actually increase the effectiveness of those dollars.

4. Just because you get something doesn't mean you have to give something. Organizations—on the level and otherwise—often give an unsolicited gift or an invitation into a sweepstakes with the expectations of a donation. Resist the urge to reward that and, instead, decide if that charity is part of your philanthropic plan.

5. Don't trust phoning fundraisers. Sure, some are okay. But if they are making a cold call to you and interrupting your day, you are under no obligation to speak to them. Again, do not provide personal information. If you do decide to talk and you do like what you hear, ask them to send information or point you to a place online where you can learn more and make a donation. Do not make any donation by phone.

6. Ask about tax deductibility. Why not take the tax break that comes with a charitable donation? Just make sure you get a receipt and try to keep all of those receipts together along with a record of the charity, the date, and the amount you provided.

7. Insist that the charity not release your personal information. Some charities make additional money by selling your information to other solicitors. Do you really want your name and number being passed around as a "generous donor?"

8. If you are dealing in the big bucks, seek professional assistance. It's too easy to be taken advantage of when you have a combination of generosity and inexperience in philanthropy. If the numbers you have to offer are large, seek the guidance of a financial planner with expertise in that area.

9. Don't take their word for it. Many solicitors will say that you've donated in the past. If the organization doesn't sound familiar, check your records.

10. Always buy from the kid who's going door-to-door selling stuff for school fundraisers. Not only is your purchase of overpriced wrapping paper, trash bags, or candy bars helping the school, it's also helping teach the young person social and professional skills.

"I HAVE
NEVER LIKED
WORKING.
TO ME A JOB IS
AN INVASION
OF PRIVACY."

–DANNY MCGOORTY

Arts & Leisure

Remember what it was like to get tested on the books you were reading? Remember when going to a weekend music festival meant a very groggy Monday at work? Now the downside of such artistic endeavors practically disappears, leaving you time to relax and enjoy the fruits of creative folks' labors.

READ THAT BOOK.

No, not just any book. Read that book you've been putting off. Maybe you've been enamored with the musical *Les Misérables* and have long wanted to check out the source material. Perhaps a trip to Dublin made you wonder what James Joyce's *Ulysses* is all about (good luck with that one). Or maybe you've got a few hefty historical biographies just waiting to be cracked. The key here is finding what you actually enjoy. Read a chapter or two and still not into it? Plowing forward may keep you from putting it aside and finding another book that you actually like. Don't be afraid to move on.

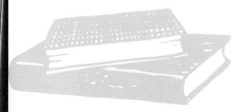

WRITE THAT BOOK.

For years you've been saying that you have a book in you. Now it's time to actually write it. Whether it's a memoir, work of fiction, narrative nonfiction, or cookbook, there's a difference between wanting to be a writer and wanting to write. Anyone can talk the talk. The trick is to get it all down on paper. Then to ruthlessly edit, rewrite, and shape it into something you can proudly set loose on the world. Where to start? The same place every writer starts...with a blank page. Need inspiration? Millard Kaufman, one of the creators of Mr. Magoo, had his first novel published when he was 90!

> What story would
> you like to share?

ATTEND MORE LOCAL EVENTS.

Yes, the big-name concerts and Broadway touring companies may get most of the media attention. But every city has its own events, sometimes a notch down in quality but often, surprisingly, even better than their big-ticket brethren. And local festivals are a terrific, low-key way to get a sampling of local talent, crafts, and food. Check in with your city, regional, or state visitors center for a list of the whats and whens.

*B*ECOMING A CINEMATIC COMPLETIST.

Whether you love John Ford westerns, Martin Scorsese crime films, or MGM musicals, surely there are films that have slipped through your lifetime of movie viewing. Now is the opportunity to create your own film festivals, filling in the blanks in genres and by those talents who you've spent a lifetime enjoying.

*A*TTEND A FILM FESTIVAL.

If you prefer a more social experience, then how about hitting a film festival? You could finally get to one of the big ones—Sundance in Utah, Telluride in Colorado, South by Southwest (SXSW) in Texas—or find one closer to home. Not only do you get to see films before they hit Netflix, but you can also meet the filmmakers who created them. Sign up to volunteer for even greater access and more opportunities for socializing and education.

What do you look for in a good movie?

*A*TTEND A MUSIC FESTIVAL.

When was the last time you spent a weekend enjoying your favorite genre of music? Whether that's jazz, folk, bluegrass, or rock and roll, there's a festival out there catering to your musical taste. Not only are you likely to see some of the top names in the field (literally *in the field* at some fests), but you also can sample musicians that aren't yet on your radar, discovering new paths to musical pleasure. Some festivals are located in cities with easy access to hotels. Others have opportunities for camping, whether in tents, campers, or RVs.

Usher.

Yes, ticket prices for plays and concerts can be high. But not for ushers. While some facilities have full-time or part-time paid staff members handing out programs and guiding patrons to their seats, others make use of volunteer ushers. In most cases, ushers can take a seat right after the curtain goes up or the concert starts, so you miss very little of the onstage action.

10 Fun
(and not depressing)
MOVIES
ABOUT
SENIORS

When you're in need of a quick flick
or an evening in, why not curl up
with these beloved classics or some
fantastic new approaches to seniors
living their lives to the fullest!

1. *Cocoon* (1985) — A group of seniors find the alien equivalent of the fountain of youth in this spirited yarn.

2. *The Lady in the Van* (2015) — Maggie Smith plays a woman who has been, yes, living in a van for 15 years. Of course, it helps that Smith can do no wrong on screen.

3. *Up* (2009) — Yes, the opening sequence is a heartbreaker. But crotchety Carl Frederickson is an animated delight.

4. *The Best Exotic Marigold Hotel* (2011) — A varied group of retirees head for the titular lodgings and the result is a very human comedy.

5. *Tortilla Soup* (2001) — Hector Elizondo stars as a retired chef with three daughters whose love life is reawakened. If you like this, also check out *Eat Drink Man Woman*, the Chinese film it's based on.

6. *Out to Sea* (1997) — You can't go wrong with a Jack Lemmon/Walter Matthau movie. In this one, they play a pair of seniors working as cruise ship dance hosts.

7. *Space Cowboys* (2000) — A group of senior astronauts—you'll recognize all of them—head back into space in this adventure.

8. *Creator* (1985) — This fanciful tale was savaged by critics, but Peter O'Toole is charming as a doctor learning to let go and live.

9. *Le Concert* (2009) — A former Russian maestro hatches a scheme to reunite his former orchestra for a gig in Paris 30 years after the group was forced to disband. It may not sound like a comedy, but it is. And the music is glorious.

10. *Young at Heart* (2007) — A senior citizen chorus covers music from Hendrix, Coldplay, and more in this inspiring documentary.

"EVERY DAY THE INCREASING WEIGHT OF YEARS ADMONISHES ME MORE AND MORE, THAT THE SHADE OF RETIREMENT IS AS NECESSARY TO ME AS IT WILL BE WELCOME."

–PRESIDENT GEORGE WASHINGTON

Working (on your terms)

Yes, you've retired from your career job. But that doesn't mean that you need to leave the ranks of the employed. For some retirees, working still brings enormous satisfaction. But now that it's optional, you should be in a better position to define the parameters of your new work life...and take a different kind of pleasure in it.

WORK AT AN AMUSEMENT PARK.

You don't have to score the role of the Mayor of Main Street, USA, at Walt Disney World to take pleasure in helping other people have a good time. Amusement parks can be great places for seasonal, and often outdoor, work with rejuvenating opportunities to work with—and have a positive influence on—young people. In addition to the obvious greeting, retail, ticket-taking, and bus or shuttle driving work, amusement parks can also be places to make use of your mechanical skills, gardening talents, and more.

*B*USINESS MENTOR.

The days of regular apprenticeships—where practical work wisdom is passed from one generation to the next—may be long gone, but mentorship is alive and well. If you aren't already well connected to an employee who might use your experience to help with job training, your local chamber of commerce is likely to have programs to make those connections possible.

What did you know when you retired that you wished you knew when you joined the company?

*B*E A PART-TIME PARK RANGER.

If your tastes are more toward the outdoors and you prefer a less hectic environment than an amusement park, a state or national park may be the place for you for a summer or other seasonal job. You've already got the 18-or-older age requirement beat by miles. Also mandatory is being a U.S. citizen and in good physical shape. Some other requirements include a driver's license and corrected 20/20 vision, with first aid and CPR training a big plus.

BE A SEASONAL CAMPGROUND HOST.

If you like camping and want to earn your site—and perhaps a bit of spending money—consider being a campground host. A host might run canoe rentals, manage the camp store, greet guests, collect fees, clean, or take care of light maintenance work. The rewards are a home away from home and a steady flow of strangers who can turn into friends you look forward to seeing every year.

START A FOOD TRUCK.

Many people have dreamed of opening up a restaurant. But perhaps it's best to leave that batch of headaches (with its inherent risk to bank accounts and sanity) to others. But with the food truck movement, there's a more modest option—setting up your own mobile food shop. Some successful food trucks are offshoots of existing restaurants, while others are stand-alones (or, rather, ride-alones). Be aware that laws vary from state to state and city to city regarding permits, inspections, where you can park, etc. Visit www.foodtruckr. com for more on the business realities, and remember that if you are interested as a hobby rather than a business, it might be best to stick to selling your wares at farmers' markets and festivals.

"THE QUESTION ISN'T AT
WHAT AGE I WANT TO RETIRE,
IT'S AT WHAT INCOME."

–GEORGE FOREMAN

$\mathcal{B}$E AN EXTRA.

Live near the centers of television and film production? If you have patience and want a story to tell your family and friends, consider signing up for one—or all—of the agencies, such as sylviafaycasting.com, that round up extras. Be warned: Much of the work consists of waiting around, and the days can be long so bring something to read and make sure your phone is charged. And if you want to find more such gigs, be particularly nice to the production assistants who will likely be your prime contacts. Just remember to leave the stars alone and that you aren't meant to be noticed.

*B*E A SANTA.

If you've got a natural white beard, why not put it to
use with the original cosplay character, Santa Claus? It
doesn't matter what your faith is, there's pleasure to be
had in hearing the wishes of kids. And a good Santa is
always in demand. Don't forget Mrs. Claus too!

Top 10 Tips
FOR TIP-TOEING BACK INTO THE WORKFORCE

Don't be afraid to get back into the game. But maybe some things have changed since you got your last job. Try these tips to ease back into it.

HELP WANTED

1. If it's been a long while since you've applied for a job, create a fresh resume.

2. Pay as much attention to your cover letter as your resume (if one is requested or expected).

3. Take advantage of opportunities to network. Use LinkedIn and other social networks not only to let potential employers know you are available but also to give them good places to learn more about you once you've applied.

4. For bigger companies, look directly on their websites for available jobs.

5. At interviews, be yourself. Don't feel the need to exaggerate your achievements. You want them to want you.

6. The basic rules still apply: Dress for the job you want, be presentable, and be early.

7. You are never too old to negotiate. If the combination of pay, benefits, environment, and the job itself doesn't meet your needs, don't just walk away. Tell them what you want.

8. Try a temp agency. Not only are the hours flexible, but you may also find yourself temping your way into a steady job once your employer sees how good you are. Then again, you may find that temping suits your life even better.

9. Don't automatically say yes if a job is offered. An offer is flattering and empowering, but make sure this is really what you would like to do.

10. Most of the above also applies to applying for volunteer work. Remember: Your time is valuable.

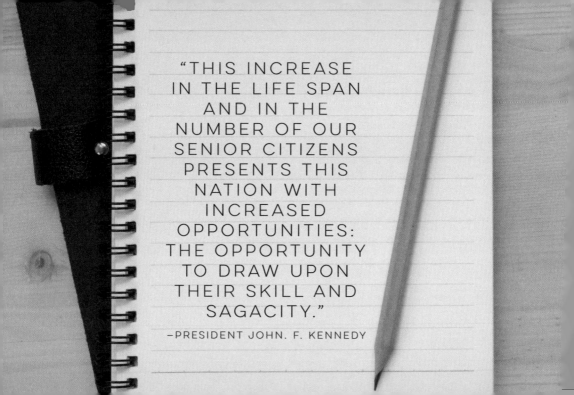

"THIS INCREASE IN THE LIFE SPAN AND IN THE NUMBER OF OUR SENIOR CITIZENS PRESENTS THIS NATION WITH INCREASED OPPORTUNITIES: THE OPPORTUNITY TO DRAW UPON THEIR SKILL AND SAGACITY."

–PRESIDENT JOHN. F. KENNEDY

TEACH AND/OR LEARN

Lifelong learning isn't just a buzz phrase. It's a way to continually grow. One of the benefits that comes with age is knowing how much there is that you don't yet know. Well, now is the time to fill in some of those gaps—where you can dictate what, when, and how deep you want to go.

GO BACK TO THE CLASSROOM AS A TEACHER.

You'd be hard-pressed to find a school district that couldn't use some committed, educated substitute teachers. But that's just one way to make use of your talents as a teacher. Adjunct faculty members make up a high percentage of the teaching corps at many colleges.

GO BACK TO THE CLASSROOM AS A STUDENT.

If Rodney Dangerfield can go "back to school" in that silly film, so can you. There is a wealth of offerings, from one-shot workshops to PhD programs available for seniors who still feel like they have something to learn. In doing so, you not only increase your knowledge and worldview but also may supply your fellow students—and your instructor—with some much-needed perspective. Some colleges and universities even offer special scholarships for seniors.

What subjects do you wish you had learned more about?

GO BACK TO THE CLASSROOM AS AN AIDE.

If you don't want to take on the full responsibility of teaching, you can always volunteer as an aide. That could mean assisting in a specific classroom, being available as a "floater" to help when needed, or serving as tutors for specific subjects. Programs such as the AARP's Experience Corps (which helps high-needs elementary students in more than 20 cities) can help guide you toward the right placement. Or check with your local school administration office.

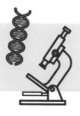 

What subjects are you most comfortable helping to teach?

EXPLORE OTHER FAITHS.

Whether you are steadfast in your beliefs, questioning the faith you were raised in, or just have a curiosity about religion and want to learn more about the great quilt of faiths that make up the world, extra time in your week could be spent attending religious services beyond your home base. Not only will you find that respectful strangers are almost anywhere, but you also may be surprised to find more similarities than differences.

*D*OCENT FOR A MUSEUM.

For some, spending more hours in museums is a desired retirement plus. If that's you—and you also have a penchant for education—consider becoming a museum docent. Some serve as tour guides, others in other educational roles. Whatever the case, they are essential parts of keeping museums active and interesting, whether it's an institution dedicated to art, science, history, or something more specific. Most docents serve as volunteers but are given museum perks. Expect a training period, which is also a great chance to meet other newcomers.

DVISE YOUR FORMER EMPLOYER.

If you've left your employer on good terms, why not negotiate a way for
you to help the business grow and improve company culture? Serving as
a business advisor can be a great way to keep your head in the game while
not being tied to stringent responsibilities.

What are some things you would like to have told your
former boss about improving the business that you didn't
feel comfortable saying while employed there?

OPEN-SOURCE YOUR SOFTWARE.

A wonderfully generous aspect of the high-tech revolution has been the contribution of independent tech-heads to software development. With open-source software, the codes are made freely available for anyone to use or improve. The movement, which began in the early 1980s, is going strong. And it's easy to become a part of if you've got the knack and have no interest in making your developments proprietary.

Close-Up:
THE RETIREMENT PARTY

A retirement party can't help but be a mix of joy and melancholy. It's a celebration, but it also marks an end, especially when your about-to-be-former co-workers are hosting the event.

Newretirement.com advises mixing the look back with a look forward, not only inviting current co-workers but also family and other folks you will be spending time with in the next phase of life. Keep in mind, too, that those you encounter daily at your workplace aren't the only people who are part of your worklife. You may not be in control of who gets invited—you may not even know the time and place when it will happen—but if you are in the planning loop, hint to the right people to consider inviting vendors, key clients, salespeople, loyal customers, and others who were important to you. Even the person who sold you java every morning from the corner coffee shop. Such key players in your worklife can make the retirement party even more special.

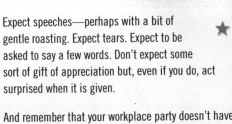

Expect speeches—perhaps with a bit of gentle roasting. Expect tears. Expect to be asked to say a few words. Don't expect some sort of gift of appreciation but, even if you do, act surprised when it is given.

And remember that your workplace party doesn't have to be your only celebration. A backyard barbecue, group trip to a minor league baseball game, friends golf tournament, Food Network-style cooking competition, or big picnic at a local park can celebrate your past while highlighting the pleasures ahead.

One safety note: If you opt to include an alarm-clock smashing demonstration in the retirement party, just remember there are a lot of parts, small and large, that can go flying. A trip to the ER certainly would dampen the mood.

Top 10 State Schools
WITH CLASSES GEARED FOR YOU

Learning doesn't have to cost a lot, even at the college level. Here are just a small sampling of the offerings available. Be sure to check the school or state's website for more details on how to enroll.

1. Delaware. Residents of Delaware over the age of 60 can attend Delaware State University or Delaware Technical Community College as formal degree candidates without paying to apply or register.

2. Hawaii. If you live in Hawaii, join the senior citizen visitor program at UH Manoa to take class for free.

3. Kentucky. Provided that the classes aren't already filled, anyone over the age of 65 and a resident of the state is admitted and enrolled without paying for tuition and other such fees.

4. Louisiana. To attend a public college or university in Louisiana for free, you only have to be 55 years old. They'll even give you a fifty percent discount on textbooks.

5. Michigan. At Michigan Tech, you can take up to two courses per semester for free if you are over 60 years old.

6. New Hampshire. The University of New Hampshire offers residents 65 or older the opportunity to attend two courses a year without paying tuition.

7. New Jersey. Rugers University offers retired New Jersey residents, age 62 or older, the chance to attend courses on a space-available, noncredit basis.

8. North Carolina. The state grants senior citizens (65 or older) up to six hours of class time and one class for no credit for free.

9. Oregon. Oregon State University allows those 65 or older to take a class when space is available and for no credit.

10. Wyoming. At the University of Wyoming, residents 65 or older can enroll for free when space is available.

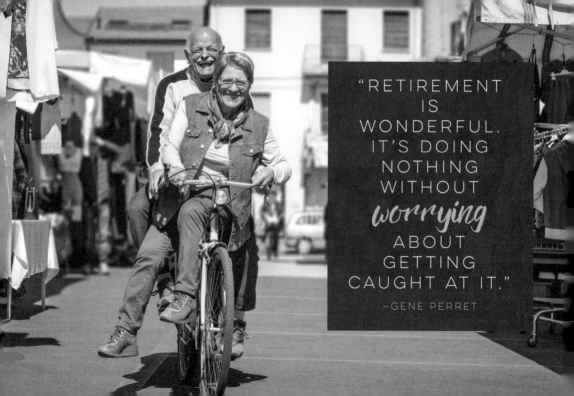

"RETIREMENT IS WONDERFUL. IT'S DOING NOTHING WITHOUT *worrying* ABOUT GETTING CAUGHT AT IT."

–GENE PERRET

IT'S NEVER TOO LATE

Now is the time to stop saying "I'm too old" or "it's too late." The time is *now* to try something new, meet new people, get in shape. There are so many ways to improve and keep your world moving— so why are you holding yourself back? Dive in!

PULL YOUR FAMILY TOGETHER.

Whether your family includes children and grandchildren or siblings and cousins—and assuming there's no raging feuds going on—bringing your clan together for a day, a weekend, or an extended vacation is a wonderful act that could ripple through generations. For those with the means, all-inclusive vacation resorts can be wonderful since you don't have to program activities or worry about meals. But you don't have to spend the nest egg. City and state parks offer shelter rentals, which are great for family reunions. And, of course, a big enough backyard and a functioning grill also can do the trick. Prepare to find out some family secrets and hear some of the same stories you've been hearing since you gathered with your grandparents.

*G*ET IN SHAPE.

No, you aren't going to ever have the body that you had in high school. But that doesn't mean you can't be your healthiest you. All the excuses that you used to have, beginning with "I don't have time to shop or cook" and heading straight through "The handball league is at an inconvenient time" go out the window. Now is the time to get on your feet, even if that means a daily leisurely walk around the neighborhood. If you haven't exercised in a while, take advantage of coaching that is usually offered when you sign up to a gym. Ease into it, find what works for you, and look forward to feeling better.

*P*LAY THE MARKET.

The same advice applies to day trading in stocks as it does in visiting the casino: Don't gamble what you can't afford to lose. That being said, with the stock market, you aren't betting against the house—which has the odds in its favor. Instead, you are betting on something, that something being a company's success. Which means you should do your homework and apply that research to making smarter bets.

FIGURE OUT WHERE YOU CAME FROM.

Only a small percentage of people know much about their family history beyond two or three generations. If your family tree seems to be pretty barren, there's no better time to fill in those branches. Thanks to the internet—which offers some pay-as-you-go options but also some free channels of exploration—you can learn a lot about your extended family. Start by asking questions of your living relatives. Then connect to those folks and keep asking. Who knows? You may find an interesting cousin or famous relative along the way.

EDIT YOUR LIFELONG PHOTO COLLECTION.

If you are like many people, you've got boxes of photos and bits of memorabilia in your attic, basement, or garage. While digging through such a personal collection can be bittersweet (or, sometimes, just bitter), wouldn't you rather create your visual life story rather than have someone else do it after you are gone? It can be a matter of simply taking a box at a time into your living room and separating the true keepers from the rest. That doesn't mean throwing the also-rans out (though you can ditch duplicates and many photos that mean nothing to you); just mark them clearly in a separate box. From there, you can scrapbook, put them in albums, or keep them loose but in a clearly marked and preservable box. Scanning them electronically gives you a whole digital library to share with friends and family.

DATE.

Whether widowed, divorced, or never married, you'll find that retirement is actually very conducive to dating. For one, scheduling becomes far less of an issue when every day is, for dating purposes, a weekend. And you may find that connecting is actually easier now, thanks to online dating services, social networks, and the ability to more easily find interest groups that can lead to connections with compatible people. Just remember, once you are out on that first date, to avoid talking too much about past romances or marriages, don't dwell too much on the kids, and relax. (Just note: A recent study showed that the lowest rate of prophylactic use was among people ages 45 and older. Take the advice you once gave your teenagers—and be careful!)

RELOCATE.

While pulling up your stakes, thinning out your belongings, and setting up elsewhere can be a daunting task, it's actually fairly common—witness the migration to Florida among retirees. But while that southern sunny state can be paradise, it's not the only place to consider. Retirement is a great time to assess what you like and don't like about the places you've lived. It can be a chance to find the view you've long wanted from your bedroom window or the proximity to the things you love. That could mean an apartment near your grandchildren, a duplex across the street from a library, or finally getting to live in the big city where you can walk to everything you need.

JOB APPLICATION FORM

as possib

Please complete this accura
this job application.

Please either type directly in this form using or print out and
CAPITALS.

EMBARK ON A NEW CAREER.

Retirement from one job doesn't automatically mean retirement from *all* jobs. And while some pick up part-time work for social reasons or simply to get out of the house and stay active, retirement can also be a time to transition into another career, one that your life experience has set you up for. Don't be shy about networking, finally updating your LinkedIn account, and letting those in your desired field know that you are able and ready to get to work.

What, career-wise, was your road not taken?

Top 10 Cities TO LIVE IN AFTER RETIREMENT

Living on just a social security check isn't easy. Which is why your quality of life could increase by moving to a lower-cost region. U.S. News & World Report took a look at the U.S. Census Bureau and Bureau of Labor Statistics information on the costs of housing, food, transportation, healthcare and utilities in 104 metropolitan areas and came up with the following top ten places to retire if your income is limited to your social security check.

Sorry, the list doesn't include San Francisco, New York, or Honolulu.

1. *Boise, Idaho*
   Plusses: Low housing cost and bargain classes at Boise State.

2. *Cape Coral, Florida*
   Plusses: Lots of waterfront property, no state income tax.

3. *Colorado Springs, Colorado*
   Plusses: Scenic beauty and more scenic beauty.

4. *Dayton, Ohio*
   Plus: Access to many high-performing healthcare facilities.

5. *Grand Rapids, Michigan*
   Plusses: Impressive arts scene, booming healthcare region.

6. *Pittsburgh, Pennsylvania*
   Plusses: Free public transportation, outstanding sports.

7. *Richmond, Virginia*
   Plus: Significantly lower housing costs than Northern Virginia.

8. *Rochester, New York*
   Plusses: Low housing costs, lots of college activity.

9. *San Antonio, Texas*
   Plusses: Rich history, no state income tax.

10. *Spokane, Washington*
    Plus: Strong for skiing and other outdoor activities.

IF YOU ENJOYED THIS BOOK
OR IT HAS TOUCHED YOUR LIFE IN SOME WAY,
WE'D LOVE TO HEAR FROM YOU.

Please write a review at Hallmark.com,

e-mail us at booknotes@hallmark.com,

or send your comments to:

Hallmark Book Feedback

P.O. Box 419034

Mail Drop 100

Kansas City, MO 64141